RANDOM THOUGHTS OF A SEEKER

Narratives, thoughts and speculations - written especially for those under the age of forty

RAJU SUNDARARAJAN

Made with ♥ on the Notion Press Platform
www.notionpress.com

This too, is for my son Harish

Contents

SILENCE IS SUPREME

Lead a simple, sober, sensible, self-sacrificing, spartan, stoical, self-disciplined, solvent, and above all, stolidly silent life.

Silence is strength, silence is the first step to sagacity, silence is supreme.

Benjamin Disraeli said: Never complain and never explain.

COUNT YOUR
BLESSINGS

An EoD thanksgiving:

This morning I woke up from a refreshing sleep; and today, no one at home was sick; no creditor or government official knocked on my door; and I had three meals.

Thanks be to God, for His loving care and protection.

WORK AND PRAYER

Always hope for the best, yet prepare for the worst.

Pray as though today were your last day on Earth; work as though you and your work will live for eternity.

MENS SANA IN CORPORE SANO – A CYCLE

All bodily health starts and ends in the mind. Feed neither your mind nor that of others with vexatious thoughts.

USE MONEY WISELY

Good uses to which money should be put (after setting aside a portion for charity and good works)

For a house to live in, for food and medicine, and for making the life of the next generation as stress-free as possible.

ELEMENTS OF EDUCATION

Teach your child to think in unconventional ways.

Throw out the water from a cup, then ask the child what the cup now contains. "Nothing", will be the answer.

Teach the child that the cup now contains air, that air too is a "thing"; that, though invisible, it can be felt; that air is a subtle, insubstantial thing which can be shoved out by grosser forms of matter like liquids and solids.

Explain that though insubstantial, air is powerful, it is capable of sustaining life when provided, and of extinguishing it when withheld.

BE INDEPENDENT, STAND TALL

Lead a fiercely independent life. Learn to cook, to do household chores, to operate household equipment.

Learn to ride a two-wheeler, to drive a four-wheeler.

Learn how to do bank, insurance and statutory work, online, as well as by traditional methods. Learn how to keep accounts, and how to calculate and submit your income-tax return. Learn to use computers and the internet and the smartphone. Always maintain an adequate balance in your bank account and cash in your pocket. Never depend on your "near and dear" ones to do things for you. If there is dependence, there will be delay, disappointment, disgust and disillusionment.

RELIGION A LA CARTE

On account of its vastness, Hinduism cannot be understood fully; it is this vastness, however, that allows it to cater to the varied preferences and needs of its followers.

At dinner time, two kinds of meals may be ordered at restaurants. One is the fixed meal of the day, the other is "a la carte", which is where one can choose various dinner courses from a menu card which may contain a hundred items. It is not necessary to choose all the items to have a satisfying meal. One may choose just 4 or 5 items and obtain satisfaction, and one person's choices will in most cases be, to a small or large extent, different from that of another.

Similarly, Hinduism. Choose those aspects that appeal to you, and follow them, without feeling guilty that you are not following the religion in toto. Also, do not sneer at the choices of your neighbour.

The human is a complex machine comprising gross body (for action) + mind (the seat of emotions) + intellect (for reasoning and discrimination). Depending on which is the predominant constituent, the human will select different aspects of religious life. An active, energetic, healthy person will choose to go on pilgrimages, have baths at sacred places, do social service, organise charities and fund-raisings, and so on. An emotional person will obtain joy from solo and/or group singing, and from the colours and rituals of religion at home or in a place of worship. A intellectual person will find that they best like philosophy, reasoning, study and contemplation.

All roads lead to the same end, so do not consider someone else's chosen path as inferior.

In general, it may be said that there are as many major religions in the world as there are majors (i.e., not minors), since each person's choice from the menu-cards of religions will be different, as each one of us is unique as regards physical body, emotions, and intellect.

Postscript: You are naturally curious to know what I recommend from the card(s). I can only say that you will have to make the choices yourself, and that your tastes will change as you age. However, I will tell you my well-considered, personal religion. It is:

1. To understand that this universe of tangibles and intangibles, as well as all individual souls constitute the body of God. God is the supreme soul, the soul of souls, the soul of the universe, and we are the cells in God's body.

In simple words, the population of the universe is 1.

2. To thoroughly understand the law of karma and the
reason for rebirths.

3. To do a little meditation daily, preferably before 6 a.m.

4. To identify one or more favourite prayers and recite or read or listen to them at least once daily; and to pray for God's blessings when doing something important and to offer thanks as many times as possible (in one's own words).

5. To be good and do good.

6. To always strive to make others happy.

7. To take good care of one's body, to make and keep it as strong and healthy and fit and flexible and light and energetic as possible - in other

words, to possess an efficient and well-tuned machine which will be capable of rendering service to other living beings.

8. To use the planet's resources, both God-made andman-made, with restraint and reverence, to take only what is needed, leaving the rest for others.

9. To pay heed to and obey the voice of conscience, to keep in mind that this voice is what distinguishes man from other forms of life on planet Earth; also to do all things in accordance with common sense; and to adopt the golden mean in all things, and at all times and places.

10. To do one's duty, if possible to help others by exerting one's limbs, and to do one's duty as an instrument of God and to avoid all sense of doership. Also, to do work with kindness in the heart and soothing words in the lips. To understand that doing one's duty with sincerity and selflessness is a sure way to salvation, irrespective of whether one is a sage or a savage.

If you want my religion in just ten words, here it is:
Duty is Deity, work is worship, service leads to salvation.

EK GOLI EK DUSHMAN

The following citation appeared in a supplement to The London Gazette:

War Office, 27th July, 1945

The King has been graciously pleased to approve the award of the VICTORIA CROSS to:-

No. 87726 Rifleman LACHHIMAN GURUNG,
8th Gurkha Rifles, Indian Army.

At Taungdaw, in Burma, on the west bank of the Irrawaddy, on the night of 12th/13th May, 1945, Rifleman Lachhiman Gurung was manning the most forward post of his platoon. At 0120 hours at least 200 enemy assaulted his Company position. The brunt of the attack was borne by Rifleman Lachhiman Gurung's section and by his own post in particular. This post dominated a jungle path leading up into his platoon locality.

Before assaulting, the enemy hurled innumerable

grenades at the position - from close range. One grenade fell on the lip of Rifleman Lachhiman Gurung's trench; he at once grasped it and hurled it back at the enemy. Almost immediately another grenade fell - directly inside the trench. Again this Rifleman snatched it up and threw it back. A third grenade then fell just in front of the trench. He attempted to throw it back, but it exploded in his hand, blowing off his fingers, shattering his right arm and severely wounding him in the face, body and right leg. His two comrades were also badly wounded and lay helpless in the bottom of the trench.

The enemy, screaming and shouting, now formed up shoulder to shoulder and attempted to rush the position by sheer weight of numbers. Rifleman Lachhiman Gurung, regardless of his wounds, fired and loaded his rifle with his left hand, maintaining a continuous and steady rate of fire. Wave after wave of fanatical attacks were (sic) thrown in by the enemy and all were repulsed with heavy casualties.

For four hours after being severely wounded Rifleman Lachhiman Gurung remained alone at his post, waiting with perfect calm for each attack, which he met with fire at point-blank range from his rifle, determined not to give one inch of ground.

Of the 87 enemy dead counted in the immediate vicinity of the Company locality, 31 lay in front of this Rifleman's section, the key to the whole position. Had the enemy succeeded in over-running and occupying Rifleman Lachhiman Gurung's trench, the whole of the reverse slope position would have been completely dominated and turned.

This Rifleman, by his magnificent example, so inspired his comrades to resist the enemy to the last, that, although surrounded and cut-off for three days and two nights, they held and smashed every attack.

His outstanding gallantry and extreme devotion to duty, in the face of almost overwhelming odds, were the main factors in the defeat of the enemy.

Thus ends the official citation.

Further information:

1. The Victoria Cross is the highest and most prestigious award in the honours system of the UK, awarded for "most conspicuous bravery or extreme devotion to duty in the presence of the enemy". The words it bears is a simple "For Valour".

2. Lachhiman was only 4 feet 11 inches in height.

3. The firearm used by Lachhiman was a bolt-action rifle, the type which has to be worked constantly with the right hand (his blown-off hand).

4. After being wounded, Lachhiman took out his kukri, stuck it in the ground in front of his trench, and shouted:

"Come and fight; not one of you will make it past my knife."
He then waited in his trench, carefully selected his targets and shot them with unerring aim, making almost every bullet count. Not one of the enemy made it past his position.

5. After being relieved, this simple man's only complaint was that the flies swarming about his wounds were a source of annoyance to him.

6. Despite excellent medical attention, Lachhiman's right hand and right eye could not be saved.

The question that now comes to mind is:

Wherefrom springs such intense courage, tenacity, and indomitability ?

The answer may be seen in the citation itself, and it is this:

DEVOTION TO DUTY.

Yes, identify your duty at all times, in situations commonplace and extraordinary; in matters small and big; towards family and friends, towards comrades, towards society and nation, and then DO YOUR DUTY COME WHAT MAY, DUTY IS PARAMOUNT.

For some reason, doing your duty selflessly causes your back, shoulders, neck and head to become more erect than they were before, improves your gait, and boosts energy and positivity as well.

THE GREATEST GIFT

The Hindu scriptures proclaim annadhaana as the greatest gift. Annam means food and dhaana means gift.

A little reflection will show why this is so. All other gifts may leave the recipient unsatisfied. A person receiving a handful of gold coins may feel that the giver could have scooped out a bit more, or that the person ahead of him in the line got a little more. Similarly with a gift of foodgrains, or any other thing.

But, when a person is served a square meal, with a variety of edibles, there comes a point when he can take no more, he is replete, he may make even violent remonstrances that he definitely wants no more. In other words, he is fully satisfied with the gift of food, he wants no more.

Providing a meal is thus a noble and most merit-worthy act.

On the micro level it applies even to cooking for one's own family, even for just one person other than the person cooking the food. Therefore, cook with love in the heart, and serve annam with kindness and humility.

In this context, one should also mention the worst scenario as regards annam. Is it the storing of leftovers in the fridge for future consumption ? Is it the giving of leftovers to the dog to eat ? No, no, no.

The worst scenario that comes to mind is that of being nagged immediately before, or while, or immediately after, partaking of a meal, thereby spoiling the diner's appetite, enjoyment, and digestion, respectively.

Keep in mind this Elementary Alimentary Truth: It is a sin to nag a person about to eat, or eating, or having just eaten, a meal.

QUALITY

I would earnestly implore all young people starting out on a career, be it of manual work or mental work, to read John Galsworthy's "Quality". It is, in my estimation, one of the greatest and noblest pieces of writing in English. I have been reading it from the age of 16 to the age of 60+, and it still thrills and moves me every time I read it. Read it, please.

IF

One more piece I would exhort my young friends to study is the poem "If" by Rudyard Kipling - a manly, masterful poem. Read it carefully, and you will see quite a bit of the Bhagavad Gita philosophy in it - especially in the line where the word "impostors" appears, and the line above it.

MAKING OTHERS HAPPY

Have you noticed that wonderful feeling that suffuses your body and spirit when you strive earnestly to make others happy ? That is a form of energy building up within you.

This energy is actually spiritual in nature, and it can be built in many ways, but the best way to build and nourish it is by karma-yoga, that most unselfish of all yogas - the yoga whereby not only the practitioner, but others too obtain benefit, in one or more ways.

Mahatma Gandhi said: The best way to find yourself is to lose yourself in the service of others.

BREVITY AND STYLE GO TOGETHER

Have you seen an expert manual worker, say, for example, a bricklayer at work ? You will see that the hand-movements are deft, and are minimal, and are a pleasure to watch.

Likewise should speech and writing be. Use the apt words, in the proper sequence, and use the minimum number of words in a way that it gives joy and satisfaction to roll them off your tongue or pen; most certainly it will also afford pleasure to the auditor or reader.

In this connection, you cannot do better than to read the speeches and sayings of Abraham Lincoln and Winston Churchill.
One example, from the latter: Fear is a reaction. Courage is a decision.

How superbly, how succinctly stated !

The French writer Antoine de Saint-Exupery said:
Perfection is achieved, not when there is nothing
more to add, but when there is nothing left to take
away.

FOUR-LETTER WORDS

Have you noticed how many beautiful, decent, soothing, uplifting, hope-giving four-letter words there are ? Much, much more, than the vulgar star-studded variety.

See the sample list below:
able, ally, best, bold, book, calm, chum, cozy, dawn, duty,
ease, elan, eyes, fame, food, free, gain, glad, glee, grin,
grow, heal, help, holy, home, hope, idea, jest, joke, joys,
just, keen, kind, kiss, life, live, love, luck, meal, mild, neat,
nice, open, pals, posh, pure, quip, rest, rich, rose, safe, sane,
save, snug, soft, star, true, wage, warm, well, wise, Xmas,
yoga, zeal, zest ...

So too, with this world. Despite enormous evidence to the contrary, there is more good than evil in this world of ours; and people, by and large, are decent, kind, helpful, and understand that the greatest joy comes out of giving joy to others.

There is hope yet.

BE PREPARED

Only one thing is certain, and that is that we can never be certain what the next minute, the next second, is holding in store for us. Anything can happen at any time and at any place to anyone. Therefore always keep your affairs in apple-pie order and a way to achieve this is to discard or destroy all papers and things the moment they are of no more use. Avoid all clutter, minimise possessions, have a place for everything and keep everything in its place.

Also, be prompt in all payments, keep all insurance policies live, nominate beneficiaries for all your assets, reveal your passwords to one or two whom you can trust.

ENGLISH

English can be a bugbear for those who seek to learn itmerely in order to use it as a tool to further their careers, but when one looks on it indulgently and with affection as a plaything, it is a lively, frolicsome, little cub bear, full of semantic antics.

So is the case with algebra - it is a terror for the student, but a source of delight for the puzzle enthusiast.

A MAMMOTH MACHINE

The universe is nothing but a mammoth machine, an enormous engine, with billions of working parts, each with specific duties to do. What are these parts? The parts are you and me, and our friends A, B and C; indeed all thinking creatures. How does the universe function, how does it run? It runs with God as the producer of the sparks from the spark-plug, the laws of dharma as the lubricant, and with all of us as the component working parts. In many ways, very similar to that micro-universe, the human.

As parts of the universal machine, it behooves us to do our duties as perfectly as we possibly can. Even a simple work slovenly done may set off a chain reaction which may impact the lives of thousands. When duties are abandoned or badly performed by people, the functioning of the universe as a whole is adversely affected.

See what happened when a farrier performed his duty in a slipshod manner:

For want of a nail the shoe was lost,
For want of a shoe the horse was lost,
For want of a horse the knight was lost,
For want of a knight the battle was lost,
For want of a battle the kingdom was lost.
So a kingdom was lost—all for want of a nail.

No action is so insignificant as to be impactless.

DO YOUR DUTY TO THE BEST OF YOUR
ABILITY AND AS AN
OFFERING TO MAN AND GOD.

BE RECEPTIVE TO NEW IDEAS

Always keep an open and receptive mind. When you read or learn of something new or strange or even bizarre, don't say "nonsense" and dismiss it from your mind. Remember that most of the things that we take for granted today could have been categorised as "things that can never be", a hundred ago. Be humble and accept that man does not yet know all that there is to be known, and that he never will reach that state. Not only is the universe stranger than we imagine, it is stranger than we can imagine.

A GREAT DOCTOR

On my first visit to a specialist doctor, I sat down and handed him my medical history file. I then allowed my eyes to roam about his room, then started speaking; but there being no response, I looked out of the corner of my eye and saw him, head bent, and holding his palm like a traffic cop halting traffic. A fraction of a second later, I noticed that he was studying my file with a concentration worthy of a student cramming for his final exams.

This man, at that moment, won my heart; I was sure that he would do me good. "This is the specialist for me," I resolved, "he is painstaking and thorough and sincere."

Although I met this doctor in his consulting room at a big hospital, he, as far as I could see, made use only of the administrative staff of the hospital.

Commencing the physical examination, he made use only of three things - a stethoscope, a sphygmomanometer, and the skill in his fingers. Evidently, he belonged to the school of doctors who have knowledge of medicine at their fingertips and also obtain knowledge of the patient's condition through their fingertips.

He then took his prescription sheet and a pen. Here it comes, I thought, a battery of tests and scans and procedures to be done. But my worry was baseless; he wrote down my medical history and the readings gleaned from his physical examination and prescribed a couple of medicines, that was all.

He was a man who understood that the patient entrusts his most prized possession to the doctor's care, and that the patient should not be put to more inconvenience, stress or expense than is absolutely necessary.

I came out of his office half-cured.

AKASHA

According to Hinduism, there are five great "elements", called pancha maha-bhootas, out of combinations of which, in varying proportions, everything in the universe is formed. These elements are earth, water, fire, air and ether; they are known in Sanskrit as prithvi, jal, agni, vayu and akasha.

All these elements, except akasha, may be known by one or more of the five organs of sense. Even before early humans learnt to make fire, they saw and felt agni in the form of sunrays. Vayu cannot be seen, only felt; if it were capable of being seen, we would be able to clearly see little else. Such is the wisdom of Creation.

Also, all these elements, except akasha, are matter + energy, the proportions of matter and energy being different in each element. The element akasha is pure, unadulterated energy, and nothing but energy. One may even term it as "vibrations".

Let us take an empty bucket. The word "empty" is a misnomer, since we know that the bucket contains air. Let us pour water into the bucket. Water, being grosser and more substantial than air, it drives out the air, and the bucket is occupied by water. Now let us drop stones (which are nothing but a substance having the element earth as its predominant component) into the bucket. Earth, being grosser and more substantial than water, it drives out the water, and the bucket is occupied by earth (stones).

Akasha is the most subtle and least tangible of the five elements. One might be tempted to think that it would be displaced by grosser elements, but that cannot be so, for how can a thing of nil substantiality be displaced ? Akasha, being pure energy, goes into everything, and everything abides in it. It imparts "vibrations", good, bad, or neutral, to the being or object it is in association with.

We have all had the experience of going to a place of worship or meditation and coming back with the feeling, "The atmosphere there was great, the vibrations heavenly". Yes, good and positive vibrations present in that space (or ether or akasha) were automatically "downloaded" into our minds and we were blessed with an uplifting sensation. The element akasha, as befitting its totally immaterial nature, can be known, but only by the mind. It cannot be cognized by the gross organs of sense.

We said that good vibrations were "downloaded" by our minds.
If so, did an "uploading" take place previously ? Yes, very much so, and it took place on account of all the good things done, good words spoken, hymns sung, prayers recited, good thoughts thought, good emotions felt, and good intentions resolved on, by countless people over many years, in such places of worship, meditation, holiness and sanctity.

Yes, ether or akasha, is the storing place of all events, words, thoughts, emotions and intent ever to have occured, occuring now, or to occur in the future. We keep uploading to and downloading from akasha all the time. With a prepared mind, one may download enormous knowledge, wisdom and skill from akasha. Sage Valmiki downloaded many parts of the epic Ramayana, and also the poetical skills to write it, from akasha.

Coming to more mundane things, dear reader, have you ever, mutatis mutandis, experienced this: You are in your kitchen when you have a thought - not a great or important thought, but a thought, none the less. You then go to the living room, watch TV, dust the furniture, and so on, when suddenly you wonder what the thought was that you had in the kitchen. Try as you might, you cannot recollect, then something tells you that if you were to go to the kitchen you might recollect it. You go, and the thought comes back to your mind.

Why was this so ? Because the thought was stronger in the ether in the kitchen than elsewhere, for a little time at least, and you were able to download it with ease.

Every deed done, word spoken, thought thought, emotion felt, intent resolved on, is present in akasha (ether) for immediate or future use. The brainwave that you had may not be "original"; it was probably downloaded from akasha by your prepared mind. It can be termed original only in the sense that the idea was not acquired by means of the five organs of knowledge, that is, the jnana indriyas.

Putting vibrations to practical use, you can create good vibrations around yourself, in the ether that is the envelope around your body and mind. Let us say that you have an important business meeting today. Start the day with prayer and seek God's blessings.

Do not ask for immoral or illegal things, pray that your path beeasy and your objective attained, if that be His will. Leave the final result to Him, He knows what is best. Keep your mind calm and detached, good vibrations are around you, though you may not be aware of it. Be polite and pleasant to those you meet on your way, more positive vibrations surround you. Give the cabman the fare and also a reasonable tip, and his look of gratitude adds further to the unseen positivity you carry with you.

You are at your meeting now. Be reasonable, polite, pleasant, and you will see that the person you have come to meet is kind, agreeable and cooperative. Such is the result of carrying good vibrations around you, it affects the other person too, and induces in them a willingness to cooperate. When persons with compatible vibrations meet, they develop a "chemistry", a good rapport, and dealings between them are to their mutual advantage.

Remember that the most intangible things are the most powerful; it is a universal law. Great things may be obtained from akasha, by a prepared mind; thought-transfer, energy-transfer, and even knowledge of things far distant in time and space.

To sum up, akasha is present everywhere in the universe;it is pure energy, and it imparts vibrations to everything it is in association with. Akasha is the most powerful of the five great elements.

One may think of it as the "bloodstream" of the universe, the universe being the body of God.

A SPOONFUL OF SPOONERISM

If Dr William Archibald Spooner were alive today, do you think he might have said that he enjoyed reading the well-known book HAPPY ROTTER AND THE STEAL-OFFERS PHONE ?

THE CATARACT OF LODORE

Here's a good reading exercise for your kids. Ask them to read out the poem "The Cataract of Lodore" by Robert Southey as loudly and clearly and faultlessly and fast as they can. At the end, they should ask for a glass of water - that is the acid test.

FLOOR THEM WITH A PRICELESS REJOINDER

The other day, a corpulent gentleman, who is a relative, came to our home, plonked himself in the centre of a sofa meant to seat three, spread out his arms both sides on the backrest of the sofa, and after allowing his eyes to roam about the living room, posed a somewhat inaccurate question, "How much was a square foot when you purchased this place ?". I went into details, comparing costs of yesteryears with current prices, and so on.

After he had left, the perfect answer to his question came to my mind. "A square foot, here and elsewhere, and at all times is 144 square inches, my dear sir", I should have said.

That's the trouble with me - I can't think on my feet, but have no trouble doing so with my fingers on my laptop.

GOING HOME

How is moksha obtained ? Moksha is liberation, or release from the wheel of samsara. Samsara is the cycle of birth, death, rebirth and so on and on.

In planet Earth, brought-forward karmic balances bear sweet and bitter fruit in one's present life; more importantly, one can fashion one's future by creating and accumulating karma, good and bad, by one's actions here and now. It is for this latter reason that our world is called a karma bhoomi.

However, Earth is a karma bhoomi only for those equipped with the voice of conscience - not for animals, nor for humans while they are infants, insane, or mentally under par.

When an Earthling dies with a vast accumulation of good karma, the soul goes to a higher-dimension planet (some call this a heaven or a bhoga bhoomi) for the enjoyment of the fruits of the good karma. In this exalted planet, there is enjoyment, but accumulation of fresh karma is not possible, just as it is not possible for an animal to earn karma in planet Earth. When a part of the good karma yet remains, the soul comes back to planet Earth.

(A prudent man who wants to settle in a new city with a view to making a fresh start goes with some money on his person, does he not ?). Planet Earth is a wonderful planet, a place wherefrom humans can strive for, and obtain salvation.

Here, on planet Earth, karma is earned or exhausted all the time. For example, I stand by my front gate, when a street mongrel passes harmlessly by. In a fit of peevishness, I hurl a stone at the animal, hit it, and cause it pain.

A portion of the animal's bad karma (which was probably earned in a previous existence when in human form) is exhausted by its present suffering; and the same amount is added to my stock of bad karma.

Liberation comes when the load of karma, good and bad, is drained. For this, one should avoid everything that results inaccumulation of bad karma. One should also avoidaccumulating good karma, since this will result in being sent to a heaven - which is not liberation. If bad karma is an iron chain which binds one to the wheel of samsara, good karma is a golden chain - but for all that, it is a chain.

The way out is to keep doing good, but without the sense of doership, merely as an instrument of God, and acting machine-like and without ego and as per His will at all times. This way, one will not be fettered even with a golden chain.

Have you ever heard of an author's pen or PC claiming a prize for literature ?

At the time of the soul's parting from the body, even though care had been taken to avoid all karma, a portion of good and bad karma will remain. When these are trivial in amount, they are written off by the grace of the universal bookkeeper.

The soul now has no dues to collect from or pay to the universe;it quits the marts of the universe.

Jnana marga is difficult, it can be traversed by only a very few.

An ordinary person should lead a life free of worldly desires, do selfless work as per the dictates of the voice of conscience, pray frequently for forgiveness and eradication of karma, settle all karmic dues with equanimity; then the soul goes home when it leaves the body.

About The Author

Raju Sundararajan was born in 1957 and led a fairly uneventful life for nearly sixty years. He had a stroke on the palindromic date of the year 2016 and suffered paralysis of his voice muscles and the left side of his body. After about four months of vigourous physiotherapy he resumed his profession as a Chartered Accountant and retired in 2018 after four decades of office-going life. He lives in Chennai, southern India, as part of an extended family of eight members, comprising four generations, with a male and a female in each generation.

THE END